PRAISE FOR

9 STRATEGIES TO BUILD AND GROW YOUR AUTHOR PLATFORM

"In her sweet way, Shelley Hitz blasted away the marketing guilt I carried for years. Somehow I believed people viewed marketing as flaunting pride in myself.

She has written a great training manual on how to grow an author platform, and reach a target audience that needs the content. She includes how-to examples and specifics.

I will visit this book again and again, and I recommend it, especially to Christian writers - and hopefully market without guilt.!"

- Ada Brownwell

9 Strategies to
BUILD and GROW
Your Author Platform

Shelley Hitz

Body and Soul Publishing LLC
Colorado Springs, CO

Shelley Hitz
P.O. Box 6542
Colorado Springs, CO 80934
www.shelleyhitz.com

Earnings Disclaimer: There is no promise or representation that you will make a certain amount of sales, or any sales, as a result of using the techniques that are outlined within this book. Any earnings, revenue, or results using these marketing strategies are strictly estimates and there is no guarantee that you will have the same results. You accept the risk that the earnings and income statements differ by individual. The use of our information, products and services should be based on your own due diligence and you agree that we are not liable for your success or failure.

Full Disclosure: Some of the links in this book may be affiliate links (excluding any and all links to Amazon) and we may earn a small commission when you make a purchase through them. By law (FTC), we must disclose this. However, we want to ensure you that we only endorse products and services we believe in and would or do use ourselves.

Book Layout ©2013 Book Design Templates
www.shelleyhitz.com/booktemplates

Ordering Information:
Quantity sales. Special discounts are available on quantity purchases by corporations, associations, and others. For details, contact the "Special Sales Department" at the address above.

9 Strategies to BUILD and GROW Your Author Platform/ Shelley Hitz -- 1st ed.

ISBN-13: 978-0692697412
ISBN-10: 0692697411

Download the PDF version of this book and watch the bonus video training here: http://trainingauthors.com/sellmorebooks

TABLE OF CONTENTS

Introduction

This book is all about building and growing your author platform.

The idea for this book came to me while I was in church one Sunday. Yes, I know, I am supposed to be paying attention to the pastor and not thinking about book ideas when in church. However, sometimes the best book ideas come to us at the strangest times. I bet you would agree and have a few stories of your own.

For weeks, I had been reflecting about what really works when building an author platform to sell more books. I was reading books and reflecting on my own success as an author. Then, in the middle of that church service in March, the idea came to me in the form of a 9-step formula.

My 9-step formula is contained within the following acronym:

B.U.I.L.D. and G.R.O.W.

Immediately, I realized the 9 steps contained within "BUILD and GROW" not only represents my own success as an author, but also clearly explains what every author truly wants. We want to build an author platform that connects us with our potential readers—our customers. And once we have built our author platform, we want it to grow.

Building and growing our author platform will allow us to accomplish two things:

1.) Reach more people with our message.
2.) Sell more books.

However, so many times we get stuck in the process.

I have talked with many authors over the years, and so many of them get stuck in one step or another of building an author platform.

In this book, I am going to give you a step-by-step system that can help you connect with your readers so that you can get more exposure and sell more books. Sound good?

What is an author platform?

Many authors are confused by the term "author platform." To explain this, let me use the following illustration.

I performed a lot growing up, so I was often on a platform. I would sing in the children's choir at church and was cast as the lead role in a musical in eighth grade. In high school, I was in show choir and performed in a singing group in college.

However, if we had performed without a stage, on the floor with everyone else, or if there had been no lights or sound system, it would have been very difficult for the audience to get the best experience possible. It would have been difficult for them to see or hear us.

For performers, the platform brings you up to a level where everyone can see you and hear your message.

The same thing is true for your author platform. It allows you to gain the attention of your target audience—to get noticed and get exposure.

Your author platform is the stage.

Simple or complex?

Your author platform does not need to be complex. It can be simple to get your message across.

For example, sometimes a street performer uses a small box and stands on a street corner. That is their platform. In a similar way, your author platform can be simple, but effective.

However, you can add another way to reach your audience with your author platform. Just like popular music artists will rent a big stadium, use all kinds of lights, have the best-of-the-best sound equipment, and smoke machines to reach their audience, you can also create a more complex way to reach your target audience. There is an entire spectrum; you can have something very simple or something very complex. Whatever you choose, you need to have an author platform.

When done properly, it can provide a way for you to reach your audience, gain exposure for your books, services, business, and eventually build trust with your audience where they want to buy from you.

And that's the end goal, right?

We want our message to reach more people. We want to earn an income from our work. It is the difference between writing as a hobby and writing as part of a thriving business.

The steps I share in this book are strategies I wish I had known when I first started publishing in 2008. What I am going to share with you is what I have learned the hard way.

They say hindsight is 20/20, right?

I have made many mistakes in my career as an author, but I persevered. In 2011, I resigned my 9-to-5 job as a physical therapist, and have been working full-time as a self-employed business owner (author, speaker, and entrepreneur) since that time. I have published over 40 books and continue to publish new books all the time. If you are interested, you can read my full bio, including my successes and my failures, at: http://www.shelleyhitz.com/about-shelley-hitz

This short book is not meant to be a comprehensive guide containing every detail you need to learn regarding book marketing. However, its purpose is to give you the foundational framework for which you can build the rest of your book marketing efforts upon. Building an author platform is a long-term strategy that can reap rewards for years. I've sold over 103,000 books in the last six years, and I feel like I am just getting started!

And now I am excited to take you on this journey of building and growing YOUR author platform.

Let's get started!

B – Bridge to Your Readers

The first part of the BUILD and GROW system is to build a bridge to your readers. I want you to see your author platform as a bridge to your readers. Your platform allows your readers to find you. For example, imagine how different things would be if we did not have any physical bridges. We literally could not get to certain locations.

My husband and I were missionaries in the country of Belize for two years. During our stay in Belize, we took a trip to Blue Creek in the Toledo district. This was one of the poorest areas of the country, and at the time, they had gotten a lot of rain. Therefore, we had to cross several bridges to get into the town, Blue Creek.

One of the bridges we had to cross was almost submerged. Had that bridge been completely underwater, we would not have been able to get across. We would not have been able to get our message to the people in that village that evening. We had a big Suburban with big tires, and so even though there was several inches of water, we were still able to get across.

Is your book an island?

I want you to ask yourself these questions:

- Do your readers know your book exists?

- Have you built any bridges to connect your book with your readers?
- Do you have any way for your reader to find you?
- Do you have a website?
- Do you have social media platforms and other ways to connect with your reader?

If you didn't answer "yes" to most or all of those questions, it will be very difficult for your readers to find you.

I want you to think about how you are creating a bridge to your readers with your author platform. You are creating a way to reach your reader.

There are three essential components of your author platform.

Your website

Your website is the first essential part of your author platform. I recommend you have a website as your hub. Your website should be the place you promote online and offline to your target audience.

Here is a list of the pages you should include on your author website (the first five are essential, the last four are optional)

1. Homepage
2. About
3. Book pages
4. Contact page with a form

5. Email list signup page

6. Blog – A page for your blog posts, if you choose to blog

7. Resources – Apart from your About page, your resources page will be one of your highest visited pages on your website.

8. Events – Speaking events, etc.

9. Media page – Links to press releases/interviews, links to download a press package (headshot, bio, etc.)

Not every author needs to have a blog. It may not be the best use of your time. However, blogging can be an effective strategy, especially for non-fiction authors, to get traffic to your website.

If you do choose to blog, I recommend you keep your website and blog under the same URL. This way, if someone lands on a blog post, they will see the navigation to the rest of your website pages. It also makes it easier to manage.

Social media

The second essential part of your author platform is social media. When I mention social media to authors, I can tell many of them feel overwhelmed. However, you can keep your social media marketing as simple as you need to in order to get your message to your audience.

In the social media realm, I recommend authors choose one or two platforms to focus on. If you try to do everything, it is easy to get overwhelmed. Focus on one or two social media platforms and spend time interacting on those platforms. That way, you can build stronger relationships with your followers on those platforms than if you try to do it all.

I know most authors want to spend their time writing. Therefore, building an author platform is not usually a very high priority. However, a lot of authors are not selling many books.

I want you to think about building bridges to your readers. It is going to take time, but think about it as a long-term investment.

Email marketing

The third and final part of your author platform is your email subscriber list. This is where you offer something of value for free to your target audience in exchange for their email address.

Building an opt-in email list has been my most effective marketing strategy. I will talk more about this part of your author platform in the section on "I – Invite."

Why should you invest time into building an author platform?

An author platform allows you to sell more books. I have built an author platform both for my books for authors, as well as my Christian non-fiction books.

Because of the work I have put into building my author platform, I can launch a book successfully with very little work, simply by sending out a few emails to my subscriber list and posting on social media.

There is power in building a platform.

You can reach more people with your message, sell more books, and even attract the attention of publishers. If you want to have your book traditionally published, publishers want to see that you already have an established platform before offering you a contract.

I believe building an author platform is essential for long-term success for all authors.

Section Recap:

- B = bridge
- Your author platform builds a bridge to your readers so they can find you online.
- The three essential components to your author platform are your website/blog, social media platforms (1-2), and an email list.

U – Understand Your Target Audience

If you want to sell more books, influence readers, and create a business from your books, you will need an audience. Otherwise, you could end up frustrated and give up on your dream altogether.

I don't want that to happen. I don't want you to give up. I want you to keep going forward with the purpose that God has for your life.

Just like you need a blueprint when you build a house, I strongly recommend you have a blueprint when you build an author platform. Even if you haven't published your first book, you can start building your author platform now. Remember, this is a long-term strategy, and so the earlier you start, the better. Actually, I recommend starting it as soon as possible—even before your first book is published.

Your strategy for building your author platform comes from understanding your target audience.

The "U" in BUILD and GROW represents understanding your target audience.

Who is your ideal reader? I'll give you a hint: it is not everyone. A lot of authors want to say, "Everyone is my target audience."

However, you need to target your audience:

- Gender: Women or men?
- Age: 22-65? Young adults ages 12-18?
- Interests: Does your audience have certain hobbies?
- Beliefs: Sometimes your target audience will have specific religious beliefs or political affiliations.
- Who is your audience, and where do they hang out online? Where do they spend their time?

For example: Are they spending time on Instagram? A lot of teenagers are on Instagram. Are they on Facebook? My primary audience spends a lot of time on Facebook. Therefore, I have chosen to spend a lot of my time there.

What does your target audience want?

> Fiction: They want to be entertained. They want to be able to escape for a little while.

> Non-fiction: They want to learn something new. What information do they want to know? What is their main problem and how can you help them solve it?

It is important as you are building your author platform to understand your target audience and to know what it is they want.

Section Recap:

- U = Understand your target audience
- Find out more details about your target audience (i.e., gender, age, interest, beliefs).
- Where does your audience spend time online? Find out, and then spend a majority of your time there.

I - Invite

The The next part of the BUILD and GROW your author platform strategy is "I": Invite.

When building a relationship with your potential readers, it is important to invite them into your space. Instead of forcing your book upon people who are not interested, I want to encourage you to share your book with those who are interested in what you have to offer—after they have given you permission to contact them.

The best way to do this is through an email list. And I am not referring to collecting emails and sending a group message through your regular email provider, like Gmail or Yahoo. In order to comply with spam laws, you need to use an email service like:

- GetResponse – www.trainingauthors.com/getresponse
- Aweber - www.trainingauthors.com/aweber
- TrafficWave -www.trainingauthors.com/aweber

I have used all three, and they are all great services.

Benchmark email is free to get started and includes autoresponders if you have a tight budget. Getresponse and Aweber has the best support staff. And TrafficWave is the best value as you get unlimited subscribers for one low price.

When you invite someone to sign up to your email list, I recommend giving them an ethical bribe, something for free, in exchange for signing up to your list.

Fiction authors

For example, a fiction author might give away three chapters of a book as a PDF download. However, what I highly recommend is writing a short novella specifically for your email newsletter list. When you write this novella, don't publish it anywhere else. Therefore, the only way your fans and readers can get that novella is if they sign up for your email list.

Non-fiction

For non-fiction, your free gift can be a resource list, guide, tutorial, etc. What is the main pain point of your target audience? What is something they want? Then give it to them— something short and sweet. You can provide a PDF report, a video, or an audio file.

Permission-based marketing

Once someone signs up for your email list, they have given you permission to continue to contact them. They can unsubscribe at any time; however, as long as they stay subscribed, they are giving you the right to be in a relationship with them. The foundation of marketing is all about building relationships where your target audience grows to know, like, and trust you.

It is similar to playing catch. Let's say you ask someone to play catch with you and they are inside their house and are not interested. If you force them to play catch with you, there is going to be damage that occurs to their window when you throw the ball to them. It will cause damage to the window.

However, if they open their window and show interest, you can start playing catch. As their interest grows, they may even come outside with you to continue playing catch.

Similarly, when you invite someone to connect with you online and/or sign up to your email list, some will be interested and others will not.

However, some people are going to say, "Yes, I am interested. I want to find out more." Then they may want to eventually buy your books, services, or other products you sell.

The biggest advice I have for authors is to not force yourself upon people who are not interested. It can cause damage. When authors constantly send the message "buy my book," it will turn people away.

You could stand out on a corner with a megaphone, and shout your message. But, we all know this method can get annoying. Or, you could be invited to someone's home for coffee. They have given you permission to come into their home. You can sit in their living room and share your message to them over a cup of coffee.

Which is going to be more effective?

Talking to the person when they have given you permission, right?

I see so many authors struggling with this right now. Many are shouting, "Hey, look at me, look at me. Buy my book, buy my book." And it's not working.

But, an email system can give you permission to continue the conversation with your target audience. And that permission can make all the difference.

Automate what you can.

Part of your email marketing can be automated. All of the services I mentioned have autoresponders you can set up to go out automatically to those who sign up to your list. I think about it as having a virtual assistant that helps you 24/7. I recommend setting up five to seven different autoresponder messages from the beginning, and then continue adding new ones as you can.

Set up your autoresponder messages to go out at least one a week so that your subscribers remember who you are and yet not too often to be annoying. These messages should be evergreen. This means they are not going to be time-sensitive, and you will be able to share this same message for months or years with your list without needing to update it.

Send out one-time broadcast messages.

I also recommend you send out one broadcast email per week for non-fiction authors, and one broadcast email a month for fiction authors.

A broadcast email can be time-sensitive to let your audience know about special sales. Or it could simply be an email to let them know the progress you have made on your novel, links to interviews you have recorded, etc.

I encourage you to share something personal as well. Letting your followers know about your personal life can make a huge difference. How much you share is up to you.

Similar to an email list, when people like your page on Facebook, when they follow you on Twitter and other social media platforms, they are also giving you permission to share more with them. However, I recommend considering an email list as the number one way you invite your target audience into your space.

Section Recap:

- I = Invite
- Use an email service (GetResponse, Aweber, Trafficwave) and invite your target audience to sign up by giving something of value away for free.

- Schedule 5-7 autoresponder messages to be sent once a week.
- Send one broadcast message per week for non-fiction and/or one broadcast message per month for fiction.

L – Link Together With Others

The "L" in BUILD and GROW is link together with others. When we work together with other people and network, it can be extremely powerful. I have seen this to be true.

Building relationships with others in your niche can be a win-win for everyone. Reach out to influencers to find out how you can work together. I recommend that you offer to do something for them first. How can you help them? How can you serve them?

When you are introduced to an influencer's audience, you get exposure to their established platform. This can yield great results when done properly and is especially helpful for unknown authors just getting started building their platform.

Guest Blogging

For example, guest blogging is a great option for connecting with powerful influencers in your area of expertise. What you can do is approach different bloggers and offer to write content for them.

Many bloggers will even tell you when they are going to be at a conference or on vacation. Those are great opportunities to offer to write a guest post for their blog, as they may need to schedule content while they are away. You want to make sure your post is appropriate for their audience and you want it to be unique content that has not been published anywhere else. This is your chance to make a first impression to their audience, so I encourage you to put your best foot forward.

Usually this will be a one-time opportunity, but occasionally blogs will invite you to be part of their team of writers. For instance, I am a guest blogger for TheFutureofInk.com and write a post for them every month. This has been great exposure for me and gives me credibility as an expert in my field, as I am writing alongside other experts in the publishing and marketing niche on that site.

When you can write a guest post on a popular blog, you can potentially get your message to thousands of people that already follow that blog. And at the end of your guest post, you should have a byline or a short bio that says something about who you are, and includes a call to action. I usually recommend having that call to action include asking people to sign up on your email list.

For example, here is an example of a byline/bio I have used:

> Shelley Hitz is an award-winning and internationally best-selling author. She is the owner of TrainingAuthors.com and is passionate about helping authors succeed in publishing and marketing their books.
>
> She teaches from personal experience. Shelley has been writing and publishing books since 2008, and

has published over 40 books including print, eBook and audio book formats.

Download Shelley's free training "Building a Book Marketing Plan" ($27 value) when you sign up for her newsletter here:
www.trainingauthors.com/newsletter

Interviews

Another option to link together with others in your genre or niche is to be a guest on their podcast, Google+ hangout, or online radio show. Look for opportunities to be interviewed on popular shows in your niche. Similar to blogging, you will be introduced to an established audience filled with your target reader.

If you were sharing the message of your book in a stadium, you would want that stadium to be filled with those interested in your topic or genre, right? You can have the most amazing book; however, if your stadium is empty, you will not sell many books. You need to fill your stadium by building traffic to your website and converting visitors to email subscribers. One powerful way to do this is to connect into someone else's established platform.

Try this twist on interviews.

I used this technique with a different twist when I first launched my website for authors. I hosted a telesummit with book marketing experts on the topic of Facebook marketing. I aligned myself as an expert as I interviewed these established experts. Plus, the speakers did some marketing—they sent information to their followers on how to access the telesummit. This helped build my list and also successfully launched my paid Facebook product after the telesummit ended.

Everyone has to start somewhere.

In the beginning, as you build your platform, you will only be connected with a few people. Everyone starts with zero email subscribers, zero blog followers, and zero social media connections. Normally, your platform will build slowly over time. Therefore, you want to think of creative ways you can connect, network, team up with, and build relationships with influencers in your niche: those that are powerful and already have an established platform filled with your target readers. It is powerful when you can plug into someone else's established platform.

Section Recap:

- L = Link together with others
- Find popular blogs and offer to write a guest post for them.
- Find a list of over 650 blog hosts here:
- www.trainingauthors.com/bloghosts
- Approach hosts of popular podcasts, Google+ hangouts, and online radio shows about hosting you on their show.

Pitch an idea relevant to their show and something of value to their listeners.

- Consider hosting your own interviews with experts in your field.
- Come up with other creative ways to connect, network, team up with, and build relationships with influencers in your niche

D – Deliver Amazingly Helpful Content

The next part in the BUILD and GROW acronym is the "D," deliver amazingly helpful content – or as my colleague Kim Roach says, "Deliver epic content." You want to be able to have something of value to share with your audience. You want to be helpful. You want to offer solutions to your readers' problems. Offer great content on your blog, email list, social media, and you will begin to build your tribe of followers.

If you are a fiction author, that means you are offering a way for your readers to connect with you outside of your book. Maybe you're sharing excerpts of your books, interviews, or introducing them to other great authors. But you are delivering amazingly helpful content.

One of our most popular posts on our blog is one where I share my 11-step checklist and 76 places to submit a free KDP select promotion (www.trainingauthors.com/47-places-to-submit-your-free-kdp-promotion-for-your-kindle-ebook/). Because the post was developed over years of real-life experience and offers tons of helpful resources, people link to it and come back to it again and again.

When you deliver helpful content, people will naturally be attracted to you. You will become a resource person and expert they look to for answers. You will be a person that they go to when they need a smile for the day, or when they need a little entertainment break.

Section Recap:

- D = Deliver amazingly helpful content
- The more you give and serve your audience, the more you will attract your target audience.
- Brainstorm ideas for blog posts, videos, and social media posts you can create to deliver epic content.

BUILD your author platform.

Let's review what we have covered so far in building your author platform.

The "**B**" is where you build a **B**ridge to your readers. The basic construction of that bridge is your website/blog, your social media platforms, and your email list. Those are the roads that will lead people to you and to your books.

The "**U**" is **U**nderstanding your target audience, knowing who you are trying to reach.

The "**I**" is **I**nviting your target audience to give you permission to market to them. You invite them to sign up for your email list, follow you on social media, and so forth. Therefore, you are NOT the person on the side of the corner with a megaphone. Instead, you are the person sitting in their living room, having coffee with them, and becoming a trusted friend/advisor.

The "**L**" is for **L**inking together with others. This is important, especially for new authors. Make sure you don't miss this part of the BUILD and GROW formula.

And finally you have the "**D**," which is **D**elivering amazingly helpful content. The more helpful you can be and the more you are serving your audience, the more you are going to attract loyal fans and followers, who eventually become customers.

That is the basis of BUILD. Next, we are going to cover how to GROW your author platform. Once you have the basic framework in place for your author platform, you can start investing your time and energy into growing your audience.

G - Give

The "G" in BUILD and GROW is simply...give. As I discussed in the previous chapter on delivering amazingly helpful content, I encourage you to make it your goal to serve others. Instead of being focused on yourself, your book, your sales, I encourage you to focus on others.

- How can you help your readers?
- How can you serve influencers in your niche?

A self-centered approach to marketing will repel people away. For most authors, this approach will not feel good over time. You may have even experienced this yourself. I have talked with authors who dread book marketing because they see very few results from their efforts and it seems as if no one is listening to them. Many times, this is the result of forcing their book and their message upon people who are not interested.

The good news? Book marketing doesn't have to be that way.

When you have a message to share, whether it is a fiction book that entertains or a nonfiction message that inspires or educates, you are helping someone. Instead of seeing marketing as self-promotion, I encourage you to see it as one way to help your target audience.

And when you do not market your book, your message does not get to that person that needs it. They will not have your solution to their problem, or they will not be entertained and inspired.

Change your paradigm and the way you see book marketing. It is not about "YOU, YOU, YOU." Instead, marketing is all about helping your target audience. When you can start to make that switch in your mind, it can do amazing things for the success of your marketing efforts.

Being other-centered in your marketing will offer a breath of fresh air, both for you and your target audience. Your target readers are going to be attracted to you. They are going to build a relationship with you where they grow to know, like, and trust you. And eventually, they are going to wonder....

What are you going to publish next? I want to buy your next book!

Section recap:

- G = give
- Be other-centered in your marketing instead of self-centered.

R - Results

Next, the "R" in BUILD and GROW is results. This is what marketing is all about: getting results. However, I know so many authors – and believe me, I've been this way, too – who do not evaluate their efforts. This chapter is all about evaluating your results. I like to call it testing, tracking, and tweaking.

Marketing is all about testing: testing what works and what does not work. Although you don't want to get burdened with statistics and numbers, they can give you a lot of clarity when you know what is working and what is not.

Without knowing your numbers, you will be marketing in the dark. Knowing your numbers will shine a light on where you are getting the best return for your investment of time and money. Most of the time 20% of your efforts will produce 80% of your results. Once you know what's working, you can then focus even more on that strategy or technique.

For example, if you are spending a lot of time on Pinterest, and after six months you see very little return on your investment of time, you need to change something. You will either need to tweak how you are approaching marketing on Pinterest, or consider changing your focus to a different social media platform. However, you will not know what is working and what is not if you don't track it.

I recommend taking time once a week to track your book marketing efforts. Track your book sales, blog statistics and social media followers. See where people are coming from when they visit your website. Are they coming from Pinterest? Are they coming from Facebook?

You can track the clicks on the links you post on social media as well. One way to do this is to use SmartURL to create a link. You can create a different link for each place you promote or use their advanced tracking system.

See more here: www.trainingauthors.com/are-you-losing-customers-over-this-common-problem

To get results, you need to continue marketing.

Make sure you continue to do something every week to promote your book. I have so many ideas for you to do that. What I recommend is that you create a monthly calendar, and on that monthly calendar, choose a one-time promotion idea to implement for the month.

One-time promotions would include:

- Planning a book launch
- Paid advertising
- Scheduling interviews on podcasts, Google+ Hangouts
- Guest blogging
- Speaking engagements
- Etc.

In addition to your one-time promotion activity, choose one ongoing promotion activity to focus on for the month.

Ongoing promotions would include:

- Blogging (on your own blog)
- Video marketing (e.g., YouTube)
- Podcasting
- Social media marketing
- Etc.

I recommend every author develop a habit of marketing on social media. It does not have to be tons of time; you can invest just 15 minutes a day.

Whatever you do, get into the habit of doing something every week to promote your book and tracking your results.

Section recap:

- R = results
- Start a simple system to track your book sales, website visitors, and social media followers on a weekly basis.
- Continue doing something every week to market your book.
- Plan out a monthly book marketing calendar with one-time promotional and ongoing promotional activities.

O - Offer

The "O" in the BUILD and GROW formula represents your offer. Although you are not going to want to use the "buy my book, buy my book, buy my book" speech all the time, you are going to want to offer something of value and ask your target audience to buy it. If you never ask them to buy, you most likely will not get many sales. Just like the Bible says, "You have not because you ask not." I believe a lot of times the same is true in our marketing.

Although we do not want to be on the one extreme where we're pushing, pushing, pushing and trying to get people to buy, we also do not want to swing to the other end of the spectrum, where we never ask our target audience to buy – even those who have given us permission to market to them. You still do need to ask your readers to buy through an offer.

Remember, they have already given you permission to send them an offer when they signed up for your email list. Now it's time to ask.

You want to make it your goal to give more than you take, so I recommend your marketing messages be 20% offers and 80% giving information. Some of you may watch my marketing and realize I don't always follow the 80/20 rule perfectly myself; sometimes I'm more 50/50. However you do it, you want to make sure you are asking your followers to buy what you have to offer. Otherwise, you will not sell many books.

Section recap:

- O = offer
- Ask your followers to buy your book, product, or service through an offer.
- Try to follow the 80/20 rule where you offer something to buy 20% of the time and offer great content 80% of the time.

W – Write More Books

The last and final part of the BUILD and GROW formula is the "W," and that's simply represents writing more books.

I have personally found no other technique more effective for marketing my books that to write more books. The more prolific I am as a writer, the higher my book royalties. Not only do I have more books to sell to new customers, but I also have new books to offer for sale to my existing customers. This is powerful. Once you build a platform of fans and followers, you can share your newest book to them via your email list and immediately see new sales rolling in. As you write more books, you will have a snowball effect.

Consider writing a book series.

I want you to consider writing a series. If you have written a book on a certain topic, consider writing a series around that topic. Or if you are writing fiction, consider writing a series. Then all of your books will cross-promote your other books within each book. And if you have written a series, each book will be very closely related. Therefore, the person who buys one book will most likely be interested in buying the other books in your series.

I love the way my colleague Kristen Eckstein does this. She has a series for authors called the Author's Quick Guide (www.trainingauthors.com/booksbykristen/) series. Then she puts all of her covers in one big graphic and includes the call to action, "Collect them all." So if you have bought one or two of her books, there is a good chance you will be interested in buying the other books in her series.

I have written several series of books. I have a series called The Book Marketing Survival Guides that my co-author Heather Hart and I wrote. I have a series on gratitude, A Life of Gratitude with four books. I have a series on faith, A Life of Faith, with four books– and so forth.

See more here: www.trainingauthors.com/books and www.shelleyhitz.com/series/a-life-of-gratitude

The bottom line? Keep writing more books.

As writers, we don't want to be spending so much of our time marketing that we are not continuing to write. Publishing more books is an incredible way to be able to sell even more of your existing books.

Let's recap the entire BUILD and GROW your author platform formula.

BUILD =

"**B**" is being a **B**ridge to your readers.

"**U**" is **U**nderstanding your target audience.

"**I**" is **I**nviting them into your space through an email list, social media, etc.

"**L**" is to **L**ink together with others. When you tap into established platforms that already have a hungry audience that are your target audience, it's a powerful way to gain more readers on your author platform.

"**D**" is **D**elivering amazingly helpful content.

GROW=

"**G**" is where we continue to **G**ive, give, and give. I know it seems like the opposite of what you think you should do; you should be selling, right? However, when you give, I really believe you will receive.

"**R**" is **R**esults. Make sure you're tracking your results. What's working, and what's not? Wisdom is knowing when to persevere and when to let go.

"**O**" is the **O**ffer. You want to eventually then offer something to your readers to buy.

"**W**" is to **W**rite more books.

There you have it! My 9-step formula to BUILD and GROW your author platform. When you put these strategies to work, it's a long-term strategy for success to increase your exposure, to get your message to more people, and to sell more books.

Now, it's your turn.

I'm cheering you on,

P.S. As you know, reviews are gold to authors. If you have found this book helpful, would you consider leaving an honest review on Amazon.com? You can find it here:

www.amazon.com/dp/B00OD40ZU4

Bonus Video Training

Download the PDF version of this book and watch the bonus video training here: www.trainingauthors.com/sellmorebooks

Earnings Disclaimer

There is no promise or representation that you will make a certain amount of sales, or any sales, as a result of using the techniques that are outlined within this book. Any earnings, revenue, or results using these marketing strategies are strictly estimates and there is no guarantee that you will have the same results. You accept the risk that the earnings and income statements differ by individual. The use of our information, products and services should be based on your own due diligence and you agree that we are not liable for your success or failure.

Full Disclosure: Some of the links in this book may be affiliate links (excluding any and all links to Amazon) and we may earn a small commission when you make a purchase through them. By law (FTC), we must disclose this. However, we want to ensure you that we only endorse products and services we believe in and would or do use ourselves.

About the Author

Shelley Hitz has coached thousands of authors through her books, training programs, online events, seminars, and more. She has over a decade of experience speaking to groups of all sizes, from small workshops to keynote presentations in front of thousands. However, she is best known for injecting energy and enthusiasm into everything she does and inspiring those around her to take action.

Her clients are successfully publishing new books almost every day and some have become #1 Amazon best-selling authors within days of publishing their books simply by following her proven system.

Learn Shelley's 6-Step "ASCENT Method" she has used to write 40+ nonfiction books FAST.:

www.shelleyhitz.com/freetraining

Connect With Shelley Online!

Facebook: www.facebook.com/authoraudience
Twitter: www.twitter.com/shelleyhitz
YouTube: www.youtube.com/shelleyhitztv

See a complete list of Shelley's books here:
www.shelleyhitz.com/bookshelf

www.ingramcontent.com/pod-product-compliance
Lightning Source LLC
Chambersburg PA
CBHW060523280326
41933CB00014B/3080